Ian Holloway

Ian Holloway is a former professional football player and manager from England. He was born on March 12, 1963, in Kingswood, Bristol, England. Holloway played as a midfielder during his playing career, representing several clubs, including Bristol Rovers, Wimbledon, and Queens Park Rangers.

However, Holloway is perhaps best known for his managerial career. He has managed several clubs in English football, including Bristol Rovers, Queens Park Rangers, Blackpool, Crystal Palace, Millwall, and Grimsby Town, among others. Holloway gained widespread recognition for his colorful personality, eccentric quotes, and passionate approach to the game.

One of Holloway's notable achievements as a manager was guiding Blackpool to the Premier League in the 2009-2010 season. Despite being one of the smallest clubs in the division, Blackpool played an exciting brand of attacking football under Holloway's leadership and won promotion through the playoffs. Although they were eventually relegated, Holloway's tenure at Blackpool was highly regarded.

Throughout his managerial career, Holloway became known for his distinctive post-match interviews, where he often delivered entertaining and humorous quotes. His charismatic personality made him a popular figure among football fans and the media.

Known for his colorful personality and quick wit, Ian Holloway became a popular figure in English football. His post-match interviews often captivated audiences with his humorous and offbeat comments, earning him a reputation as one of the game's most entertaining personalities.

During his managerial career, Holloway had varying degrees of success with different clubs. He enjoyed a successful spell at Blackpool, leading the team to promotion to the Premier League in 2010 and narrowly missing out on a return to the top flight in the following season's playoff final. Holloway's attacking style of play and the team's underdog status endeared them to fans across the country.

After leaving Blackpool, Holloway went on to manage Crystal Palace and achieved another promotion to the Premier League with the club in the 2012-2013 season. However, Palace struggled in the top flight, and Holloway departed the club in 2013.

Holloway later managed Millwall, where he helped the team reach the League One playoffs. He also had a short stint at Grimsby Town, where he took charge in 2019 but left the club in 2020.

Throughout his career, Holloway's passion for the game and his ability to connect with players and fans made him a popular and respected figure. His unique approach to management and his infectious enthusiasm endeared him to many supporters.

Although Ian Holloway is no longer currently active in football management, his impact and memorable moments continue to be cherished by fans of the clubs he worked with. His charismatic personality and entertaining interviews have left a lasting impression on the footballing community.

After his departure from Grimsby Town, Ian Holloway has not taken up any managerial positions at professional clubs. However, he has remained active in the football world through media work, including punditry and occasional appearances as a guest on sports shows.

Holloway's insightful analysis and engaging personality have made him a sought-after figure for football-related discussions. His ability to provide unique perspectives and his knack for delivering memorable quotes continue to entertain and engage audiences.

In addition to his media work, Holloway has also expressed his passion for the game by involving himself in various football-related projects. He has been known to participate in charity events, coaching clinics, and motivational speaking engagements, where he shares his experiences and knowledge with aspiring players and managers.

Throughout his career, Holloway has left a lasting impact on the footballing community. His passion for the game, his ability to inspire players, and his entertaining persona have made him a beloved figure among fans. His contributions as both a player and a manager, as well as his charismatic presence in the media, have solidified his place in the history of English football.

While Ian Holloway's current endeavors may not be widely known, his influence and legacy within the sport continue to be recognized and appreciated. His unique approach to management and his ability to connect with people through his personality have made him a memorable figure in the footballing world.

Playing career

After his initial playing stint at Bristol Rovers, Holloway joined Wimbledon in July 1985 for a transfer fee of £35,000. However, his time at Wimbledon was short-lived as he was sold to Brentford in March 1986 for £25,000. He spent just over a year at Brentford before joining Torquay United on loan in January 1987, where he made five appearances.

In August 1987, Holloway returned to Bristol Rovers, who were playing their home games at Twerton Park in Bath at the time. Under the management of Gerry Francis, Holloway thrived at Bristol Rovers. He had an impressive four seasons with the club, missing only five games during that period.

When Gerry Francis was appointed as the manager of QPR (Queens Park Rangers) in the First Division (now the Premier League) in 1991, he brought Holloway to the club as one of his first signings. In August 1991, Holloway joined QPR for a transfer fee of £230,000. He spent five seasons at QPR, making over 150 appearances for the club.

In August 1996, Holloway returned to Bristol Rovers for the third time, but this time as a player-manager. He took on the dual role of managing the team while still being an active player. This marked the beginning of his transition into football management.

Managerial career

When Holloway took over as manager of Bristol Rovers, the club was facing difficulties both on and off the pitch. However, in his first season in charge, Holloway guided the team to a 17th place finish in Division Two (now League One). It was a stabilizing season for the club under his leadership.

The following season proved more successful for Bristol Rovers, as they secured fifth place in the league, earning them a spot in the playoffs. In the playoff semi-finals, Rovers held a first-leg advantage of 3-1 against Northampton Town. However, in the second leg, they suffered a 3-0 defeat, resulting in a 4-3 aggregate loss and elimination from the playoffs.

The 1998-1999 season ended with a somewhat disappointing 13th place finish for Bristol Rovers. However, it marked a transition point for Holloway as he retired as a player at the end of that season. Holloway had amassed over 400 appearances for Bristol Rovers throughout his playing career.

With his playing days behind him, Holloway could now fully focus on his managerial responsibilities. In the 1999-2000 season, his last full season at Bristol Rovers, the team finished 7th in the league, narrowly missing out on a playoff spot. It was a promising campaign, but they fell just short of securing a place in the promotion playoffs.

Queens Park Rangers

In February 2001, Holloway was appointed as the manager of Queens Park Rangers (QPR) during the 2000-2001 season. His primary objective was to keep the team in Division One (now the Championship). Unfortunately, QPR finished second from bottom and were relegated to the third tier of English football for the first time in 34 years.

Despite the relegation, Holloway remained in charge and embarked on rebuilding the squad. In the 2001-2002 season, he managed to stabilize the team's performances, and in the following season, 2002-2003, QPR narrowly missed out on promotion.

Holloway's efforts paid off in the 2003-2004 season when he guided QPR to promotion back to the second tier. The team finished second in the league, behind Plymouth Argyle. This achievement marked a successful turnaround for QPR under Holloway's management.

In his first full season in the Championship, Holloway led QPR to an 11th place finish, which was considered respectable. The following season, 2005-2006, QPR continued to hover around mid-table under Holloway's guidance.

However, on February 6, 2006, Holloway was suspended (sent on gardening leave) by Queens Park Rangers. The club's board stated that the constant rumors linking Holloway to the vacant managerial position at Leicester City were causing too many distractions for QPR. Ultimately, Leicester City appointed Rob Kelly as their manager, while QPR finished 21st in the league, narrowly avoiding relegation.

These details provide further insight into Holloway's tenure at Queens Park Rangers, including their relegation, subsequent promotion, and his eventual suspension. Thank you for sharing this additional information about Ian Holloway's time at QPR.

Plymouth Argyle

On June 28, 2006, Ian Holloway was appointed as the manager of Plymouth Argyle, where he expressed his ambition to take the club to the Premier League. His tenure at Plymouth started on a positive note when the team secured a 3-2 victory over Sunderland in an away match on August 12. To celebrate his first away win as manager, Holloway offered to buy a drink for every one of the 700 fans who made the 805-mile round trip.

However, there were rumors and press speculation regarding Holloway's future at Plymouth. On November 21, 2007, Holloway submitted his resignation to the Plymouth Argyle board amid speculation that he was about to be offered the vacant managerial position at Leicester City. The Plymouth board responded by stating that he was still under contract and his resignation would be considered on November 23. Eventually, a compensation package was agreed upon, and Holloway was announced as the new manager of Leicester City on November 22, signing a 3.5-year contract.

Holloway's departure from Plymouth Argyle was met with negativity from the club's fans, as they were disappointed with his decision to leave. Holloway later reflected on his time at Plymouth and admitted that leaving the club was the biggest mistake of his life, acknowledging that he had neglected the values of honesty, trust, and loyalty that were instilled in him by his parents.

Leicester City

Ian Holloway made history at Leicester City by becoming the first manager in over 50 years to win his first league game in charge. The team secured a 2-0 victory over Bristol City, marking a positive start to Holloway's tenure.

However, tensions arose between Holloway and Plymouth Argyle when the two clubs faced each other. Ahead of a match against Plymouth, Argyle chairman Paul Stapleton criticized Holloway for allowing several high-profile players to leave Plymouth before joining Leicester. Five players had left Plymouth during the January transfer window, and Stapleton placed the blame on Holloway. The comments stunned Holloway, and his lawyers looked into the statements. Leicester City chairman Milan Mandarić defended Holloway and accused Stapleton of "sour grapes," emphasizing the achievements Holloway had made during his time at Plymouth.

In the match between Leicester and Plymouth, Holloway's former club emerged victorious with a 1-0 win. The result added to the tense situation surrounding Holloway's departure from Plymouth and his move to Leicester.

Leicester City's 2007-2008 season did not go as planned, and they won only nine out of 32 games. As a result, the team was relegated from the Championship, entering the third tier of English football for the first time in their history. This marked a significant moment for Leicester City, a club that had previously been a part of the top two tiers for the majority of its existence.

On May 23, 2008, after Leicester's relegation, Holloway and the club mutually agreed to part ways. Reflecting on his time at Leicester, Holloway expressed his devastation about the club's relegation and acknowledged the support of the fans. He wished everyone connected with Leicester City well for the future and stated that the club would always remain close to his heart.

Blackpool

On May 21, 2009, it was reported that Holloway would be announced as the new manager of Blackpool, and the appointment was confirmed later that day. He signed a one-year contract with the club. His first league game in charge was a 1-1 draw against his former club, Queens Park Rangers, on August 8, 2009.

After nine months, Holloway guided Blackpool to the Premier League by winning the playoffs. The team finished sixth in the Championship and secured promotion. This achievement made him only the second Blackpool manager to win promotion in his first full season, with the previous manager being Les Shannon in 1970. Holloway considered it the best moment of his life, aside from seeing his children born.

In late July, Holloway led Blackpool to victory in the South West Challenge Cup, which was the first time a Premier League club had participated in the annual pre-season tournament.

Before Blackpool's first top-flight season in 40 years, there were media reports suggesting that Holloway was set to resign due to a dispute with club chairman Karl Oyston. However, Holloway denied the rumors at a press conference and described his relationship with Oyston as "absolutely fantastic." He clarified that he had been attending a Premier League meeting and welcomed the arrival of new players at the club.

The following day, it was reported that Holloway had signed a new two-year contract with Blackpool. Despite some challenges, such as a fine imposed by the Premier League for fielding what was believed to be a weakened team and the eventual relegation from the Premier League after one season, Holloway continued to lead the team.

He marked his 100th game in charge of Blackpool with a victory over Ipswich Town on September 10, 2011. In May 2012, Holloway guided Blackpool to the Championship playoffs for the second consecutive season, but the team lost 2-1 to West Ham in the play-off final.

During his time at Blackpool, Holloway had a win percentage of 37.8% in league games, with 54 wins from 143 games.

Crystal Palace

On November 3, 2012, Holloway agreed to join Crystal Palace as manager, although caretaker manager Curtis Fleming remained in charge for the match on that day. Holloway took charge of his first game on November 6, which Crystal Palace won 5-0 against Ipswich Town.

On May 27, 2013, Holloway guided Crystal Palace to promotion to the 2013-14 Premier League. They achieved this by beating Watford 1-0 through a penalty converted by Kevin Phillips in extra time.

However, in the 2013-14 Premier League season, Crystal Palace struggled initially, only managing to secure three points from the first eight games. As a result, Holloway came under pressure to keep his job.

On October 23, 2013, after a 4-1 loss against Fulham, Holloway left Crystal Palace by mutual consent. This departure came less than a year after he took charge of the club.

Millwall

On January 7, 2014, Holloway signed a two-and-a-half-year contract with Millwall. He took charge of the club and successfully guided them to Championship safety for the 2013-14 season, with Millwall finishing 19th in the league, four points above the relegation places.

However, in the following 2014-15 season, Millwall found themselves in the relegation places in the Championship. Holloway acknowledged that he had become an unpopular figure among Millwall fans. The team's poor form and position in the league put Holloway under increasing pressure.

On March 10, 2015, after a 4-1 defeat at home to Norwich City, Holloway was sacked by Millwall. This marked the first time in his managerial career that he was dismissed from a position. At the time of his departure, Millwall were second from bottom in the Championship and had lost five of their last six games.

On November 11, 2016, Holloway made a return to Queens Park Rangers, taking over as manager for a second spell, replacing Jimmy Floyd Hasselbaink. He stepped into the role with the aim of guiding the team back to success.

During his tenure, Holloway implemented his tactical approach and sought to improve the team's performance. However, his second spell at QPR was not as successful as his first. He faced challenges in terms of results and consistency, and despite his efforts, the team struggled to achieve their desired level of performance.

On May 10, 2018, Holloway and Queens Park Rangers decided to part ways. The decision was made after a period of reflection and evaluation of the team's performance. Holloway's departure marked the end of his second spell as manager at QPR.

Grimsby Town

Ian Holloway joined Grimsby Town as manager on December 29, 2019. Along with his managerial role, Holloway also became a shareholder in the club by purchasing £100,000 worth of shares. This allowed him to attend board meetings as a director in addition to his responsibilities as the club's manager.

Under Holloway's leadership, Grimsby Town initially experienced a resurgence. They won their first two games under his management, defeating Salford City 1-0 at home and Mansfield Town 1-0 away. Holloway made several signings, including his former Blackpool players Billy Clarke and Elliot Grandin, in an effort to strengthen the squad.

However, the team's progress was disrupted by the COVID-19 pandemic, which led to the early termination of the season. Holloway made changes to the squad during the summer, including bringing in loan signings, but faced challenges in terms of team performance and results.

During his time at Grimsby, there were also developments in the ownership and potential takeover of the club. Majority shareholder John Fenty announced he would step back, allowing Holloway more freedom in running the club. However, discussions of a potential takeover and conflicting reports regarding investment led to uncertainty and dissatisfaction among fans.

On December 23, 2020, Holloway resigned as manager of Grimsby Town. He cited his displeasure with John Fenty's decision to sell his shares in the club as a key reason for his departure. Holloway also mentioned inappropriate contact from a potential consortium interested in buying the club as a factor in his decision, although the consortium denied any direct contact with him. Following his departure, Grimsby Town temporarily appointed his assistant Ben Davies as interim manager.

Holloway's tenure at Grimsby Town drew criticism, both for the manner of his departure and the state of the squad he left behind. The team faced relegation back to non-League football for the second time in their history during the 2020-2021 season, and Holloway faced blame for the team's poor performance.

Furthermore, on January 12, 2021, Grimsby Town became the first English football club to be fined for breaking COVID-19 protocols after it was revealed that Holloway had played darts with some of his players at the club's training ground.

Overall, Holloway's time at Grimsby Town was marked by initial optimism, challenges during the pandemic, ownership controversies, and ultimately, relegation.

Future

After his departure from Grimsby Town, Ian Holloway expressed uncertainty about whether he would return to football management, mentioning that his appetite for the game had diminished.

However, in a podcast interview in late 2022, Holloway attributed his departure from Grimsby to the challenges posed by the COVID-19 pandemic and the inadequacy of his scouting network for operating at the League Two level. He also expressed interest in a return to management but specified that he would be interested in managing at the EFL Championship level.

In February 2023, Holloway applied for the managerial vacancy at Scottish Premiership club Motherwell and went through the interview process. However, the board ultimately chose Stuart Kettlewell for the position, and Holloway was not appointed as the club's manager.

Personal life

Ian Holloway has shown great strength and resilience in his personal life, facing challenges related to his family. His wife, Kim, battled lymphatic cancer, and they have four children together. The twins, Eve and Chloe, as well as their younger sibling Harriet, were born deaf due to a recessive gene both Ian and Kim carried. Holloway has been a vocal advocate for proper provision and education for children with disabilities, particularly those who are deaf. He has fought for their rights and has been involved in campaigning on deaf issues.

To ensure his children received the necessary education, Holloway commuted from Bristol to London during his time at QPR, and later relocated to St Albans. He learned sign language and has become a well-known campaigner on deaf issues, using his platform to raise awareness and make a positive impact.

Outside of football, Holloway has also dabbled in the self-sufficiency movement, keeping a variety of animals such as chickens, horses, dogs, ducks, and turkeys. He has shown an affinity for nature and a desire for a sustainable lifestyle.

Tragically, on October 20, 2020, Holloway revealed during a post-match interview that he had received devastating news of the suicide of one of his closest friends earlier that day. He expressed his deep sorrow and shock, emphasizing the importance of mental health and the need for support for those who are struggling.

In a heartwarming display of solidarity, fans of Grimsby Town, where Holloway was the manager at the time, started a fundraiser to support him during this difficult period. The fundraiser received contributions from fans of various clubs that Holloway had previously managed, reflecting the respect and support he had garnered throughout his career. The funds raised were donated to two charities suggested by the friend's family, showing the power of community and compassion in times of hardship.

Media career

Holloway is well known for his comments in post-match interviews, which are often quoted in the national media. His creative use of metaphors has made him one of the most popular interviewees and one of the cult personalities in English football. In June 2005 a book of his quotes, "Let's Have Coffee: The Tao of Ian Holloway", was published; and in June 2006 he came 15th in a Time Out poll of funniest Londoners. [77]

His autobiography, Ollie: The Autobiography of Ian Holloway, co-written with David Clayton, was first published in 2007, with an update in 2009. In August 2008 the Little Book of Ollie'isms was published, also co-written with David Clayton. Holloway also wrote the foreword for The Official Bristol Rovers Quiz Book, published in November 2008.[citation needed]

Holloway is an Honorary Patron of the anti-racist organisation Show Racism the Red Card. He attended an educational event at Bloomfield Road in 2009 along with then Blackpool club captain Jason Euell, who had just recently been the victim of racist abuse.[78] The pair attended the event and sat on a panel to share their opinions and experiences of racism with the audience of young people.[citation needed]

For the 2010–11 season, Holloway agreed to write a weekly column for The Independent on Sunday. For the 2012–13 campaign, he wrote for the Sunday Mirror. [citation needed] Holloway cited, in an interview to BBC programme Football Focus, that part of his decision to move to Crystal Palace was to be closer to family following the expectation of his first grandchild.[citation needed]

During breaks in his managerial career, Holloway has often appeared as a television pundit on EFL on Quest with Colin Murray.[79] In 2019 he also began his own podcast named "The Ian Holloway Podcast".[80] The podcast was put on hold whilst he spent time as the manager of Grimsby Town but following his departure he announced he was resuming his show and asked for questions to feature on his next broadcast by posting on his Twitter account. The post went viral when supporters of Grimsby Town began sarcastically asking him darts related questions in reference to his game of darts at the training field that caused the club to be fined by the EFL for breaking COVID-19 protocol, other fans also voiced their displeasure at the nature of his departure from the club and the lack of quality in the team he left behind.

Here is Ian Holloway's managerial record by team and tenure, as of 22 December 2020:

Bristol Rovers:

From: 13 May 1996
To: 29 January 2001
Matches: 247
Wins: 90
Draws: 70
Losses: 87
Win %: 36.4
Queens Park Rangers:

From: 26 February 2001
To: 6 February 2006
Matches: 252
Wins: 100
Draws: 71
Losses: 81
Win %: 39.7
Plymouth Argyle:

From: 28 June 2006
To: 21 November 2007
Matches: 71
Wins: 28
Draws: 23
Losses: 20
Win %: 39.4
Leicester City:

From: 22 November 2007
To: 23 May 2008
Matches: 32
Wins: 9
Draws: 8
Losses: 15
Win %: 28.1
Blackpool:

From: 21 May 2009
To: 3 November 2012
Matches: 161
Wins: 62
Draws: 43
Losses: 56
Win %: 38.5
Crystal Palace:

From: 4 November 2012
To: 23 October 2013
Matches: 46
Wins: 14
Draws: 14
Losses: 18
Win %: 30.4
Millwall:

From: 7 January 2014
To: 10 March 2015
Matches: 62
Wins: 14
Draws: 19
Losses: 29
Win %: 22.6
Queens Park Rangers:

From: 11 November 2016
To: 10 May 2018
Matches: 80
Wins: 26
Draws: 14
Losses: 40
Win %: 32.5
Grimsby Town:

From: 31 December 2019
To: 23 December 2020
Matches: 38
Wins: 11
Draws: 9
Losses: 18
Win %: 28.9
Total:

Matches: 989
Wins: 354
Draws: 271
Losses: 364
Win %: 35.8

Here are the honours Ian Holloway has achieved:

As a player:

Bristol Rovers: Football League Third Division (1989-90)
Wimbledon: Football League Second Division promotion (1985-86)
As a manager:

Queens Park Rangers: Football League Second Division promotion (2003-04)
Blackpool: Football League Championship play-off winner (2009-10)
Crystal Palace: Football League Championship play-off winner (2012-13)
Individual honours:

Football League Championship Manager of the Month: September 2004, August 2012
Football League Second Division Manager of the Month: February 2003, November 2003